Contents

Note Throughout the book players are referred to individually as 'he'. This should of course be taken to mean 'he or she' where appropriate.

◀ The pitcher is the most important player on the field: he is involved in every play and carries great responsibility

Foreword

The sports of baseball and softball are attracting more and more players and spectators. The U.S.A. is the acknowledged home of both games, but television coverage and the acceptance of baseball into the Olympic movement have brought them international recognition. Both sports provide healthy outdoor competition for millions of athletes – male and female, young and old – throughout the world.

Baseball is governed world-wide by the International Baseball Association, while softball is administered by the International Softball Federation; both bodies organise world championships and supply full rules of the respective sports.

This publication is designed to help those persons who have been attracted to the sports of baseball and softball and would like to understand the basics of both, in order to enjoy playing or watching them.

Don Smallwood

Baseball

Fundamentals of the game

Baseball is played between two teams, each with nine players. The teams bat and field in turn.

The object of the game for players of the batting side is to hit a ball with a bat and then move around a 'diamond', touching each of three bases in turn. A run is scored when a runner crosses the 'home plate'.

The fielding side tries to prevent the batters from scoring runs, and to dismiss them in a number of ways. An inning ends when the fielding side achieves three 'outs'.

A game consists of nine innings for senior baseball, and seven innings for juniors. The winning team is the one with more runs at the end of a game. If the scores are level, the game continues until a result is obtained.

The playing field

The dimensions of the baseball field were laid down by Alexander Cartwright in 1845. The playing area consists of two basic parts: the infield and the outfield. In addition, there are areas set aside for non-playing members of the two teams.

The infield (diamond)

Batter's box

This is the area, marked by lines, in which the batter stands while at bat.

First, second and third bases

Members of the batting side run from the batter's box and move in an anti-clockwise direction around a square, known as a 'diamond'. At each corner of the diamond (first, second and third bases) a base or sack is secured to the ground. This is a white canvas bag, 15 in (38 cm) square, and filled with soft material.

The distance between bases is 90 ft (27.4 m); this has remained constant throughout the history of the game. One reason is that the speed of an average runner going from one base to the

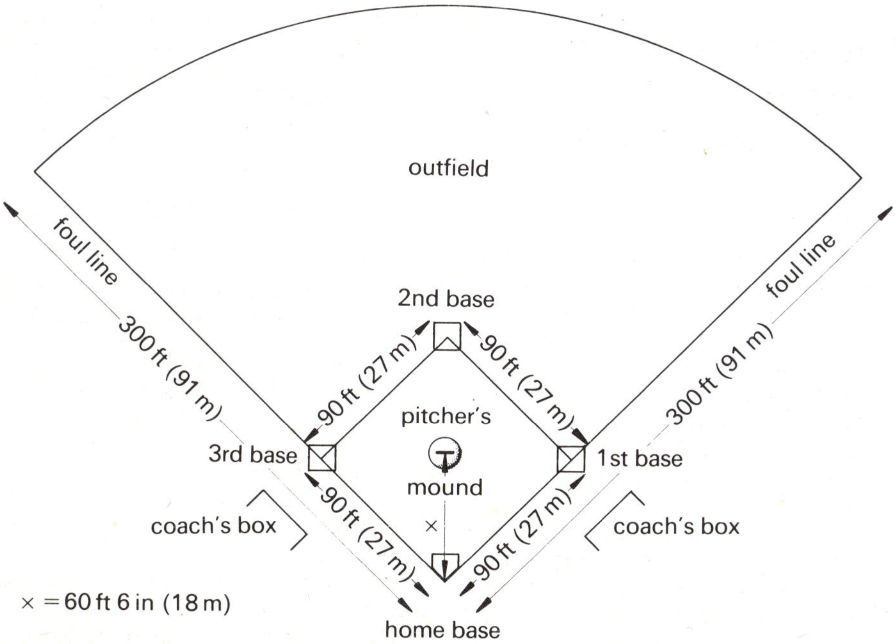

Fig. 1 The baseball field

next is equal to the average speed of a thrown ball, which results in close, exciting play on the bases.

Home plate
The home plate is the fourth and final base. It is a piece of white rubber or vinyl, flush to the ground and bordered by a strip of black. The home plate has five sides; it is 17 in (43.2 cm) wide and 23 in (58.4 cm) from front to rear, with the sharp point facing the catcher. The distance from home plate to second base is 127 ft (38.7 m).

Fair territory
This is the part of the playing field within lines drawn from the home plate through first and third bases.

Pitcher's plate
The pitcher delivers the ball to the batter from a raised mound in the centre of the diamond, 60.5 ft (18.4 m) away from the batter. The pitcher's plate is a rectangular slab of whitened rubber situated on the raised mound. It must be no more than 10 in (25.4 cm) above the level of the home plate.

Catcher's box
The catcher must take his stance within a box 43 in (109.2 cm wide), situated behind the batter's box.

The outfield

The lines defining fair territory continue through first and third bases for a distance of 250 ft (76 m) or more (325 ft or 99 m for a professional club) to the outfield fence, with flags situated at the extreme ends. These lines are called foul lines, because any ball outside them is deemed to be in 'foul territory' and therefore 'foul'.

The outfield is the area within the two foul lines.

Non-playing areas

Bench
While not active, team members, coaches and managers sit in separate bench areas, usually situated between home plate and first base, and home plate and third base. The bench is also known as the dug-out.

Bull pen
This is an area set aside for relief pitchers to warm up and practise throwing.

On deck circles
A batter who is waiting to take his turn at bat practises his batting swings in the on deck circles. These are 5 ft (1.5 m) in diameter, and are situated 37 ft (11 m) from the catcher.

Dead ball area
This extends in straight lines from the backstop net, which should be 60 ft (18 m) from the home plate, to the left and right outfield or 'foul territory'.

Equipment

The ball

The ball (see fig. 2) is a sphere with a weight of 5–5$\frac{1}{4}$ oz (142–149 g) and a circumference of 9–9$\frac{1}{4}$ in (22.9–23.5 cm).

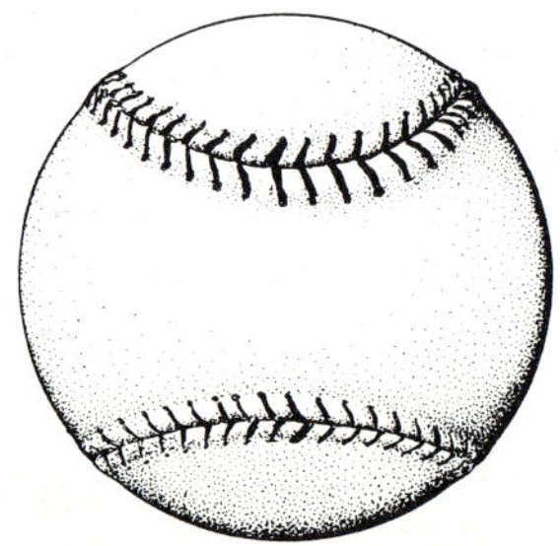

◀ Fig. 2 An official league baseball

It is made by winding yarn and laying rubber around a core of cork, then handstitching two pieces of horse or cowhide on the outside.

A smaller ball can be used for children and a softer, more durable ball is available for beginners or for use in training sessions.

The umpire is the sole judge as to whether balls are fit to be used during a game, and he removes the gloss from new balls before they are put into play. The pitcher can use the seam of the ball to curve it in the air during delivery to the batter, but the umpire penalises anyone who intentionally discolours or damages the ball by rubbing any foreign substance (e.g. soil) into it. The pitcher is not even allowed to rub the ball on his uniform, and if he is caught doing so the umpire will warn the pitcher and call a ball.

The bat

The bat (see fig. 3) is a smooth, rounded stick, not more than 2$\frac{3}{4}$ in (7 cm) in diameter at its thickest part, and not

Fig. 3 A wooden baseball bat

more than 42 in (106.7 cm) in length. It weighs about 2 lb (0.9 kg). The bat is made either of wood (liable to break while being used) or aluminium (more durable but involving greater initial outlay).

Clothing

The usual clothing consists of a baseball cap, V-necked shirt, three-quarter length trousers, socks and shoes. These are in team colours: the team's name is often displayed on the front of the shirt, while the player's name and number is on the back. Cleated shoes are permitted except in junior baseball, but the soles vary depending on the playing surface.

Protective equipment

The pitcher

The pitcher wears a padded leather or vinyl glove on his non-throwing hand.

The catcher

The catcher's protection weighs a total of 8–10 lb (3.6–4.5 kg). It includes a heavily padded glove; a helmet; a face mask with wire bars and a throat protector flap; a padded chest protector; and leg guards with extensions to protect the toes.

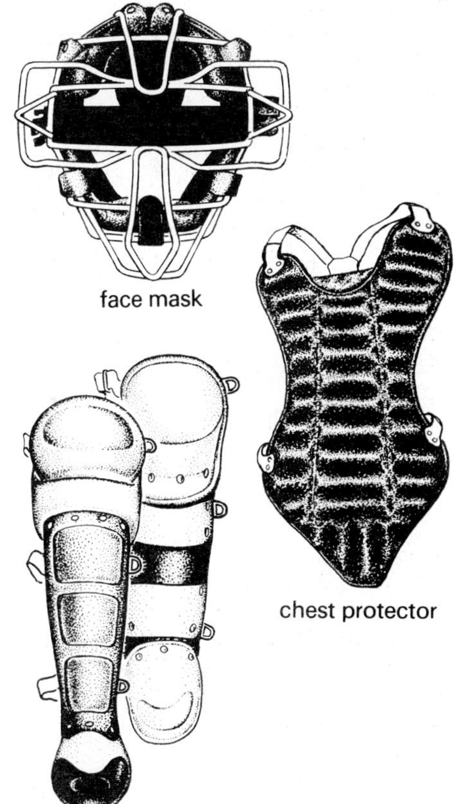

Fig. 4 The protective equipment worn ▶ by the catcher

Fielders

Other members of the fielding side apart from the pitcher and catcher wear a padded glove on the non-throwing hand.

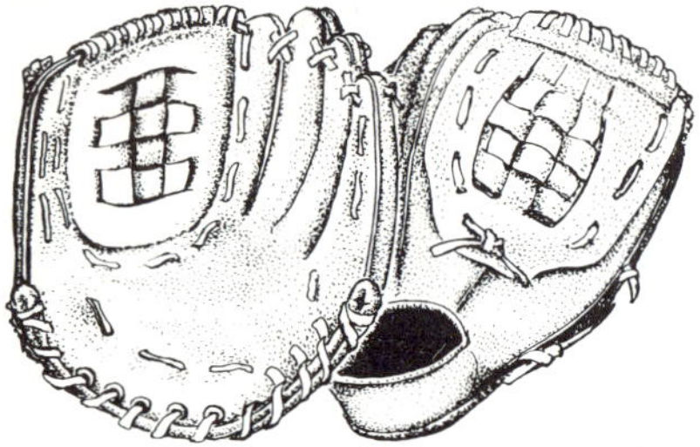

fielder's mitt

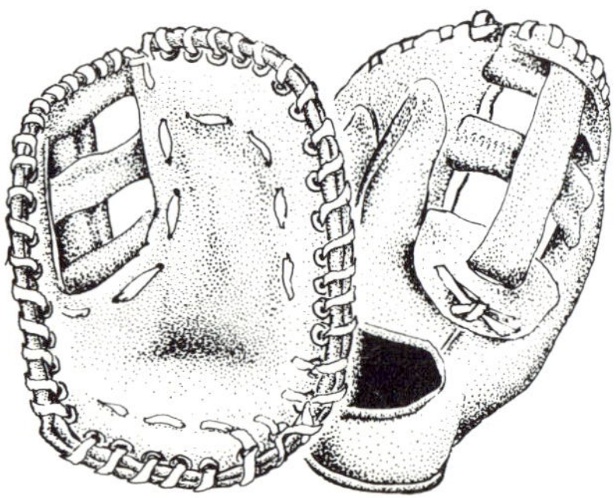

first base mitt

Fig. 5 The protective gloves worn by fielders and catchers

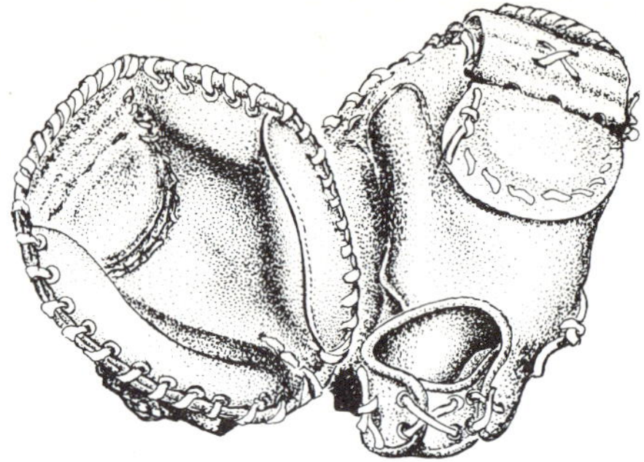

catcher's mitt

The batter

The batter must wear a helmet when facing the pitcher. Some amateur leagues extend this rule so that the helmet must also be worn when the player is running round the bases.

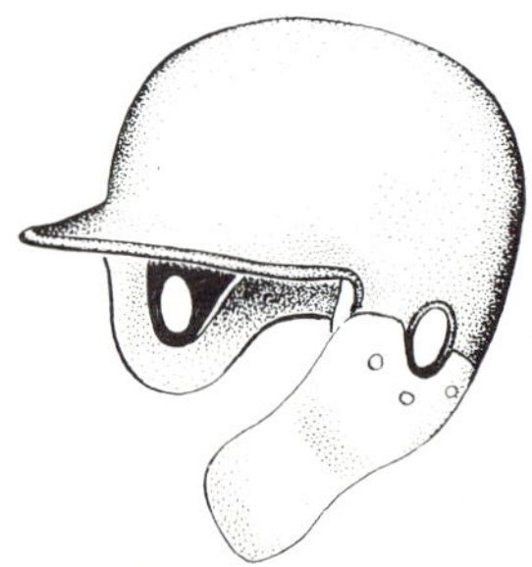

Fig. 6 The batter's helmet

Playing positions

The pitcher

The pitcher attempts to throw the ball through the 'strike zone'. This is the area over home plate and between the batter's armpits and knees. If there are no baserunners on the bases, he prepares to deliver the ball by stretching both arms upwards (the 'wind-up' position). He must then come to a complete stop before pitching the ball to the batter, with an overarm or side-arm action. When baserunners are on base, a normal overarm throw is used (the 'set' position).

When he is delivering the ball, the pitcher must have his pivot foot in contact with the pitcher's rubber; if not, 'Balk' is called by the umpire.

If the ball is pitched outside the strike zone and is not swung at the batter, it is a 'ball'. After four such balls, the batter can 'walk' to first base. See page 22 for a description of the 'intentional walk' as a defensive tactic.

◀ Great speed and deception are in evidence in this pitcher's technique

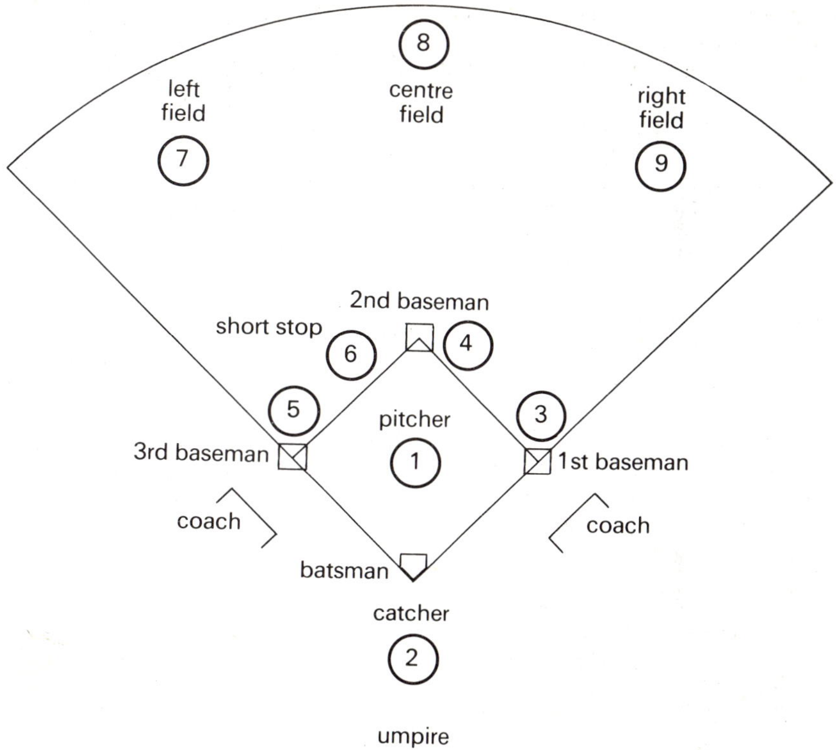

Fig. 7 Fielders' positions and number codes

Illegal pitches

a Quick return pitch: the most common illegal pitch, when the pitcher throws the ball to the batter as soon as he receives it from the catcher. If baserunners are on bases, a 'balk' is called and they each advance one base.

b Bean ball: a pitched ball aimed straight at the batter's head.

c Spitball: one that has any foreign substance on it designed to make the ball swerve or drop.

The catcher

The catcher must be positioned within the catcher's box behind home plate. His main task is to catch all pitches which pass beyond the batter. The catcher signals to the batter where in the strike zone he would like the ball to be delivered, and with what kind of pitch.

If the catcher impedes the batter in any way, most commonly if his glove touches the bat, the batter is awarded first base.

The pitcher and catcher are known as the 'battery'.

The catcher is the last line of defence and often has to show great courage to prevent a run being scored

First baseman

When a batter hits the ball, it is fielded and thrown to first base. The first baseman catches the ball in his mitt, and tries to get the batter/runner out by touching the base (usually with his foot) before the runner arrives.

Second baseman

When a runner safely reaches first base, he will be hoping to steal to second. Unlike on first base (where the baseman must touch the base while holding the ball), the runner can be 'tagged out' on second base. This simply means that the ball must touch the runner before he reaches the base. The runner will probably slide into the base in an attempt to avoid being tagged. The umpire then signals if he is 'safe' or 'out'.

If the batter hits the ball and races to first base, the runner on first base is forced to run to second ('force play'). The second baseman needs only to touch the base while holding the ball (as on first base) in order to dismiss the runner. It is then possible to throw the ball to first base and dismiss two in one play (the 'double-play').

An attempted tag out made with the runner not sliding but taking evasive action

Third baseman

The area covered by the third baseman is subject to many fast ground hits, and his ability to throw quickly and accurately to all bases can determine the outcome of a match.

Shortstop

The shortstop completes the infield. He positions himself between second and third base, and must be able to pick up the ball cleanly and throw to the bases with speed and accuracy.

The outfield

The outfield is guarded by three outfielders: left, centre and right.

The batter

The batter takes up his position in the batting box, facing the pitcher ('at bat'). He tries to hit the ball and score runs.

This player is going for a big hit ▶

The batter has three chances to hit a fair delivery from the pitcher, known as a 'strike'. A strike is called by the umpire if the pitch is over home plate between the batter's armpits and knees, and:

a the batter swings and misses

b the batter makes no attempt to hit the ball

c he hits a foul ball (except on the third strike)

d the ball hits the batter while it is in the strike zone, or

e a foul tip occurs.

The most common methods of dismissing a batter are as follows.

1. Strike-out: if a batter fails to hit the ball before three strikes are called, he is struck out.
2. Caught: if the batted ball is caught on the full by a fielder.
3. Illegally batted ball: if the batter steps out of his box to hit the ball (on fair or foul hits).
4. Impeding the catcher in any way.

5. Run out on first: if the first baseman touches his base with the ball before the batter reaches it.

The baserunner

A batter becomes a baserunner after:

a safely reaching first base after a hit, or

b receiving four balls from the pitcher.

If a batter/runner safely reaches first base by beating the ball thrown by a fielder, this is known as a 'beat-out'. Once he has reached a base ('aboard') and it is 'loaded', a runner cannot return to the base he previously occupied if the pitcher is holding the ball, has taken up his position and is in contact with the pitcher's plate.

A base cannot be occupied by two runners; the runner ahead has the right to the base. If any runner is compelled to advance to the next base because of this, it is known as 'force play'.

Fielders without the ball are not allowed to obstruct or hinder any baserunner. If a fielder throws his glove or any part of his uniform and touches a fairly batted ball, the baserunners advance three bases as a penalty.

The most common ways for a baserunner to be dismissed are as follows.

1. Forced out: if the runner is forced to advance to the next base, and the base to which he is running is touched with the ball before he reaches it.

2. Tag-out: if a baserunner is caught off his base, e.g. when he is attempting to steal to the next one.

3. Interfering with the fielder: if the runner intentionally interferes with a fielder who is completing a play. The umpire judges whether or not the interference is intentional.

4. Running outside the marked lines.

5. Passing another runner, unless that one is already out.

6. If the ball is hit into the air (a 'fly ball'), the baserunner must not leave the base he is occupying until the ball has been caught. If he does, the fielder making the catch can throw the ball to the base he should have been occupying, or the runner can be touched with the ball off the base.

Coaching positions

Base coach

The base coach is a member of the offensive team who stands in the coach's box. The first base coach advises the runner on that base, especially on stealing second. The third base coach uses arm signals to advise the runner either to stay at that base or to run for the home plate.

Manager

Each team has a manager who can play, but who is generally situated in the bench area. His judgement can make the difference between winning and losing. Team strategy, including such decisions as when to change pitchers, falls on his shoulders.

Officials

The umpires

A baseball game can be controlled by any number of umpires between one and four. They are responsible for ensuring that teams play to the rules and act in a disciplined manner at all times. An umpire's judgement is final, and he has full authority to eject from the game any person who he feels is bringing the sport into disrepute. A good umpire is one who keeps a low profile but has a thorough knowledge of the rules.

Ball

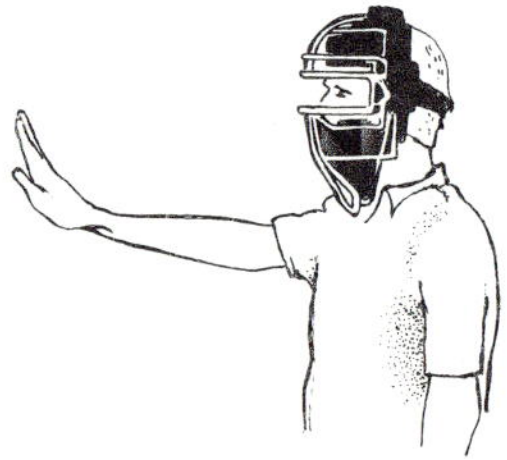

Do not pitch

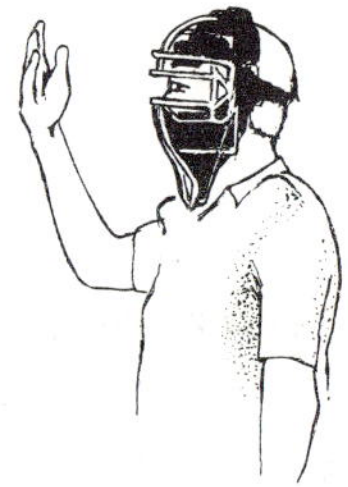

Play ball

Infield fly

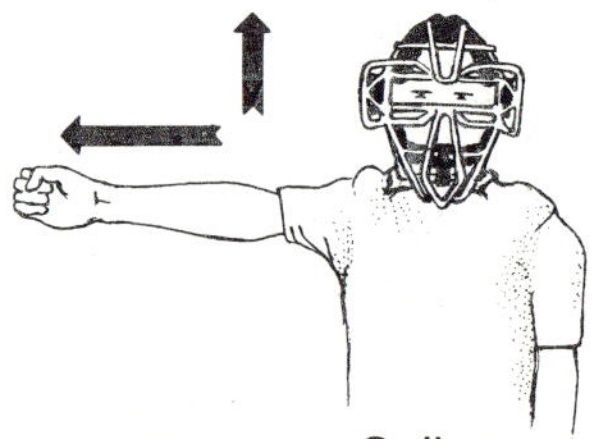

Strike

Fig. 8 Some common umpiring signals

Fair ball

Runner is safe

Foul tip

Delayed dead ball

An umpire's 'judgement call' (e.g. strike or ball, foul ball or fair, safe or out) cannot be disputed by players or coaches; for example, if a batter has second thoughts and checks his swing at a pitched ball, the umpire makes a judgement call as to whether the bat has passed over home plate into the strike zone. However, appeals can be made about interpretation of the rules.

The umpires wear a black cap, a blue shirt and grey trousers. They communicate with body signals, which are also useful for players and spectators in following the game. There is no one accepted system of signals.

Chief umpire

The 'chief' or 'home plate' umpire crouches behind the catcher of the fielding side. Because of the dangerous position, he wears a face mask (including a throat protector), a chest protector (usually worn under the shirt) and shin guards under his trousers.

The chief umpire's main duties are as follows.

1. The umpire commences play at the start of a game or after a break by calling 'Play ball' or simply 'Play'.

2. He must decide whether a delivery is a 'strike' (at a height between the batter's knees and armpits) or a 'ball' (outside these limits). The batter must hit the ball before a maximum of three strikes have been delivered.
3. The umpire uses a 'ball and strike indicator' to keep a record of the 'count' (the number of balls and strikes thrown by the pitcher to the batter). Balls are always counted before strikes, so a count on a batter could be three balls, two strikes.
4. He judges whether or not a baserunner reaches the home plate without being 'tagged'.
5. The umpire carries a small brush with which to clean the home plate.
6. Any player can request time-out from an umpire, e.g. in the case of injury. The ball is then dead.
7. The umpire can suspend the game (a 'called game'), usually because of rain or darkness. He can also end the game in the case of violation of the rules (a 'forfeited game'), with the score at 9–0 to the non-offending team.

Base umpires
Up to three 'base' or 'field' umpires cover the bases. They give decisions about base appeals for dismissal, and work as a team with the chief umpire. They shout 'Safe' to notify the runners and fielders that a runner has safely reached a base.

The scorer

The official scorer supplies the data for statistics about a particular player's performance.
1. A player's batting average is calculated by dividing his number of safe hits by the number of times he has been at bat.
2. When the catcher fails to gather a pitched ball that he should have caught, which provides an opportunity for runners to advance, he is credited with a 'passed ball'.
3. When collecting the ball, a fielder is faced with a number of options, e.g. throwing the ball to dismiss a runner who is making for first base, or a runner making for home or another base. If the latter is chosen, it is recorded by the scorer as 'fielder's choice'.
4. An 'assist' is awarded to a fielder who, while not himself making an out, has helped to do so.
5. A catch is awarded to a fielder if the ball is taken on the full and held long enough before releasing it to prove that he has control.
6. An error is credited to a fielder who makes a mistake that allows a batter to remain at bat or a baserunner to advance or remain on a base. An unearned run is one that has been scored because of a fielder's error.

Scoring

The scorecard has nine sections, one for each player in the batting order. A batter's progress around the diamond is charted by drawing a line for each base reached; a completed diamond denotes that a run has been scored.

Symbols are also used to denote how a particular batter reaches base and is out. For this purpose, the fielding team is numbered as follows: 1. pitcher 2. catcher 3. first baseman 4. second baseman 5. third baseman 6. shortstop 7. left field 8. centre field 9. right field. The method of recording outs can be demonstrated with the following example. If the third baseman fields a batted ball and throws to first base to beat a runner, this is recorded as 5–3 (third baseman (5) to first baseman (3)).

When the defensive team gains an 'out', the offensive team is 'one down'; on the next out, it is 'two down', and then 'side out'.

Scoring abbreviations

The way in which a game is reported by newspapers is called the 'box-score', segmenting it into nine innings and using abbreviations.

A.B. at bat: number of times a player batted

R. runs scored

H. hit: if a ball is batted and the batter reaches the bases without an error by the fielding side (such as fumbling the ball or throwing badly), the scorer awards a hit

R.B.I. runs batted in: when a batter hits a ball that enables a runner or runners to score runs, he is awarded R.B.I.s

H.R. home run: if the batter hits the ball over the boundary inside fair territory, he is awarded a run. A home run (or homer) is also scored if the batter hits the ball and is able to make a full circuit of the bases without stopping, touching first, second and third bases and scoring when touching the home plate. Only one run is scored, but extra runs may be scored by runners on other bases.

3B three-base hit: a hit within fair territory, after which the batter runs as far as third base

2B two-base hit: as above, but the batter runs only as far as second base

1B a one-base hit

H.P. the batter is hit by a pitched ball and walks to first base

B.B. the batter receives four balls and walks to first base

S.O. strike-out: the batter fails to hit the ball within three strikes

K. a strike-out

E.R.A. earned run average: the pitcher's average is the number of earned runs he has allowed the batting team, divided by the number of innings he has pitched.

Defensive skills

Fielding stance

The feet are spread a little more than hip-width apart; the toes point straight ahead and the body-weight is equally distributed on the balls of both feet. The fielder bends at the hips, leaning forwards with his head up and his back parallel to the ground. The hands are held palms up and fingers down, out in front of the body between the spread knees.

Catching

Whenever possible, the fielder should catch a thrown or batted ball with two hands; the fingers point downwards for a catch below the belt. The fielder should try to meet the ball with the ungloved hand and make a quick throw.

If the ball is bouncing, it should be fielded before it bounces upwards. If the ball is running along the ground, the glove should be held at ground level, as it is easier to follow a ball upwards than downwards.

Throwing

The overhand throw is the fastest and most accurate one. The side-arm throw, commonly used by infielders, is slower and has a tendency to curve.

All throws use the following action: the player looks at the target, steps directly towards it, cocks his arm (the elbow should be higher than the shoulder for the overarm throw), and follows through by bending the back.

The use of a short 'crow-hop' helps when executing a long throw: the fielder steps with the lead foot, hops on the rear foot and steps again with the lead foot.

◀ Fig. 9 The pitching sequence

Pitching

The game of baseball evolves around the confrontation between the pitcher and batter. It is the pitcher's task to prevent the batter from hitting the ball, and this is achieved partly by speed of delivery, which can exceed 90 mph (145 kph) in top competition.

However, speed is only one facet of a pitcher's delivery. A baseball has stitching on the outside and, depending on the type of grip used, the ball can be made to move in the air to produce curves and dipping deliveries. Which type of delivery is used depends on the player at bat, the game score, how many runners are on bases and how many 'outs' have been gained. The pitcher takes advice by means of the catcher's signals.

The fastball

This is pitched very quickly from the raised mound, straight to the catcher's mitt, with the object of beating the batter's reflexes and gaining a strike.

Fig. 10 Pitching grips ▶

Split-fingered fastball

With a slight adjustment of the fingers, the pitcher can produce a fast, accurate pitch that dips and falls away from the bat as it reaches home plate.

Curveball

By including a wrist action on delivery, the ball is propelled in a curved line, either from left to right or vice-versa.

Slider

A slider is disguised as a fast delivery but loses speed and deceives the batter by breaking away in flight at the point when he swings to hit it.

Knuckle ball

A knuckle ball is pitched very slowly and with no spin; its flight is irregular, moving with air currents, so that it deviates in the air in an unpredictable manner.

Screw ball

This confuses the batter by curving the opposite way to that which is expected.

Change-up

The change-up is a slower ball that deceives the batter into misjudging its speed.

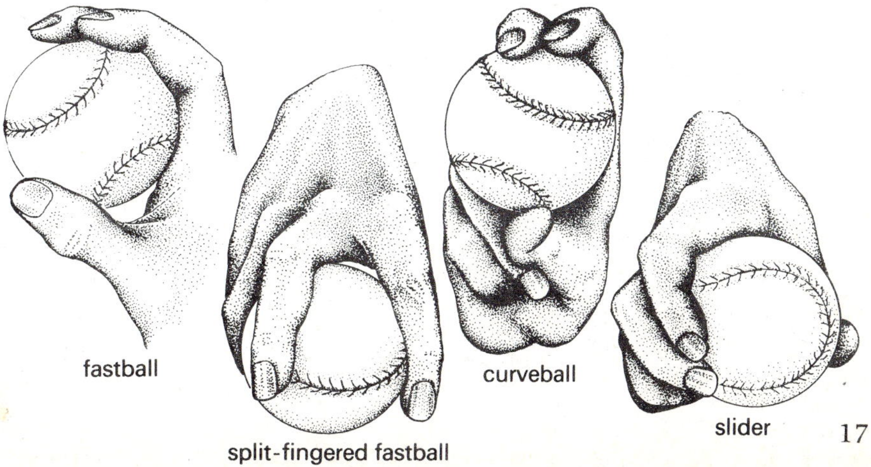

Offensive skills

Batting

A batter must be aggressive; if he is just looking for the pitcher to throw four balls, he is not going to score runs. The batter should learn his strike zone and then protect it at all costs.

To master the art of batting a player must select the best bat for himself in terms of weight and length and then learn the fundamentals of gripping the bat in order to swing it.

The essence of hitting a ball with a bat is co-ordination of hand and eye. Hitting a round object which is moving at great speed with a round bat is very difficult; when the pitcher delivers the ball, the batter has only a fraction of a second to decide whether to swing and hit the ball or leave it if it is passing outside the strike zone.

To be able to do this, the batter should adopt the following stance while watching the ball at all times. He stands with his left side towards the pitcher (if he is a right-hander), gripping the bat with both hands, with his weight on the right foot and the eyes looking towards the pitcher. As the ball approaches, he swings the bat in a curve and moves the weight onto the front foot.

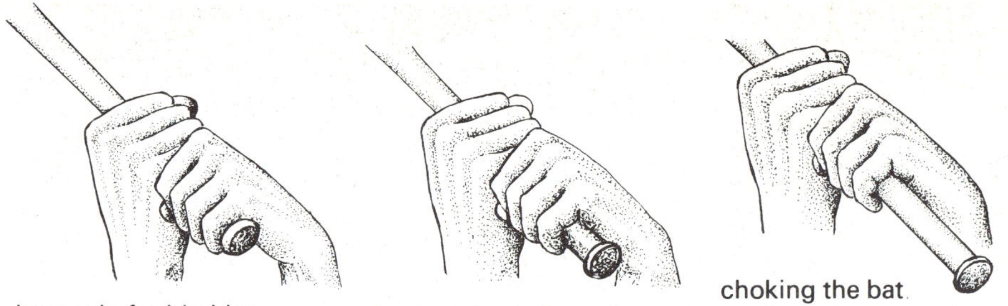

Fig. 11 Batting grips

The bat must meet the ball at the correct moment; if it is too early or too late, the ball will travel into foul territory.

Baserunning

A baserunner is basically a sprinter, and speed between bases is very important. However, while sprinting he must also be aware of the state of the game and react accordingly.

Baserunning wins games. A good, fast baserunner can tip the scales and bring victory and thus needs daring as well as speed.

He should consider how many offensive players have been dismissed, which bases ahead have runners occupying them, if the pitcher is going to attempt to throw to his base, or if a baseman is going to tag him off his base.

To obtain this kind of information, he looks for signals from the coaches who stand in their marked boxes at first and third bases in foul territory. The base coaches decide if a runner should try to steal to the next base, and signal to him and the batter that he should 'lead off' (leave his base and advance to the next). If two runners advance to the next base at the same time, it is known as a 'double steal'.

The runner here attempts to slide under the 'tag'

Sliding

Sliding into a base makes it difficult for a baseman to tag a runner, who is therefore more likely to reach the base safely. However, the runner may overslide the base because of his speed. He is then in danger of being tagged while not in contact with the base, and being declared out.

Sliding can also be dangerous, and to diminish the danger, players must be coached in the correct methods. It is important to remember that a slide is an evasive manoeuvre, and it should never be used to injure an opponent. Once a runner has decided to slide, he must never change his mind; hesitancy may cause injury.

All slides are basically the same in execution, and there are three types that are particularly common.

Hook slide

As he approaches the base, the runner stretches out his lead foot to hook the base, while the take-off foot kicks up and away from it. The arms are thrown back over the head and the whole body is flat to the ground, sliding gracefully into the base.

Bent leg slide

This is probably the most commonly used slide in the game. The runner bends his take-off foot underneath his body and slides on the foot. The lead foot contacts the base and, if a bad throw has been made, a quick recovery by the runner puts him in a position to advance to the next base.

Head first slide

If it is executed at the proper time (e.g. not when a fielder has the ball and is blocking the base), this slide is not as dangerous as one might think. The runner merely continues his running motion by leaning forwards and diving head first. He takes off with one foot and lands on his chest, with his arms out, his head up and his eyes looking towards the base.

EVANS
41
45
32

Tactics

Signals

Both the offensive and defensive teams use signs and signals, which are responsible for most tactical moves made during the game. Each team manager tries to outwit his opposite number, while coaches on the field give out many false signals to confuse the opposition. Team members must memorise the appropriate signals.

Three popular methods of signalling are the holding signal, the block signal and the flash signal.

Holding signal

This signal, which may be a closed fist, crossed legs, etc., is sustained until the play is executed.

Block signal

The body is divided so that each area represents a play. Thus, touching the belt could mean a steal, a touch of the head would mean a bunt, etc.

◀ The runner here slides head first back to first base while the pitcher 'pegs down' the runner, thus preventing him from reaching second base

Flash signal

This signal is given when the player and the coach catch each other's eye.

It is important that signals are worked out beforehand for

a instructing the batter to leave the pitched ball
b the bunt
c instructing the runners to steal a base
d the hit and run
e cancelling the play.

Defensive tactics

The defensive team relies heavily on the pitcher and his ability to beat the batter by speed and guile. Its success or failure is also dependent upon the ability of the fielders to catch the ball in the air and the ability of each team member to 'read the game'.

While it is vital that players learn individual defensive techniques, they must also know the team's defensive strategy. One such tactic might be to prevent runners from stealing bases. This is best achieved by the pitcher keeping the runner uncertain of his intentions and by the catcher throwing the ball rapidly to the bases.

The team must practise positioning for the bunt situation or the 'hit and run' attack before the game.

Balk

There are about 16 types, but the most common is the pitcher's balk, when the pitcher deliberately deceives the baserunners or batter. The umpire calls 'Balk', and the batter and baserunners all advance one base.

Pitch-out

This is a practical play by the pitcher to increase the chance of the runner being 'tagged out'. He deliberately aims outside the strike zone, to make a good batter 'walk' or help the catcher dismiss a runner who is trying to steal a base.

Infield fly

This rule was introduced to prevent an infielder from deliberately dropping a fly ball in order to trap a runner between bases. When there are less than two 'outs', with baserunners on first and second or second and third bases, the umpire calls 'Infield fly' and the batter is out. The umpire's judgement must govern, and the decision should be made immediately.

Intentional walk
If the pitcher uses the pitch-out as described earlier in order to prevent a good batsman from scoring, it is called an 'intentional walk'. The pitcher must prevent the batter from hitting the ball by intentionally pitching four balls outside the strike zone. The batter then walks to first base.

Tagging up
A baserunner must remain on the base he is occupying and wait for the catch to be made before advancing.

Relay
The use of a 'relay' in bringing the ball back into the infield is the stamp of a good defensive team. Accurate, fast throws and pre-drilled positioning of the players is essential, and calls for complete understanding between the outfielders and the infielders.

Cut-off
This play is used in many game situations and involves linking the infielders with the outfielders in order to shorten the throw back to the bases by use of a cut-off man. It can be employed when a long hit has gone out into the outfield and the infielder receives the thrown ball from the outfielder who has made the play. The infielder then acts as a 'cut-off', selecting various options depending on how far the baserunners are from the safety of their bases. Accurate throwing and speedy positioning on the part of the cut-off fielder should be a feature of a team's training programme and is the sign of a good defensive team.

Other plays brought into defensive set moves involve the catcher, the pitcher and the second baseman who, by using the cut-off play on a thrown ball from the catcher to second base, catch the runner off base and confused.

Run down
One of the most exciting plays that brings the spectators to their feet occurs when a runner is caught off-base and a 'run-down' described as a 'hot-box' takes place. This results in frenzied running and panic because the runner is helpless, and the player who has the ball should quickly and calmly size up the situation. If the runner is stationary, the player with the ball should fake a throw and run as fast as he can after the runner, holding the ball in a throwing position ready for the receiving player's call. The receiver then advances up the baseline as far as he can and prepares to call for a throw. The ball is not thrown until the receiver calls 'now'. He then catches the ball and tags the runner. If the runner has sprinted towards the next base when caught off base, the player with the ball must throw to head him off and then hold his ground for the return throw. He calls for this when he feels he can tag the runner.

The play is simple and, with practice, should always result in the runner's dismissal. Players involved in the run-down play must ensure that they move away from the play when they have thrown the ball, because if the base-runner is hindered the umpire will call 'interference' and the runner will be safe.

Offensive tactics

The batting order

Coaches and managers look for certain skills when organising the batting order.

First batter A good bunter, better than average hitter and a very good runner; known as the 'lead-off'

Second batter Should also have good speed and be able to bunt

Third batter The best hitter in the team, and a fast runner

Fourth batter The team's big hitter, who will give the runners time to score runs

Fifth batter Another big hitter, in case the fourth batter is off form; otherwise known as the clean-up batter

Sixth batter A consistent hitter

Seventh batter The most inexperienced player

Eighth batter The poorest hitter and slowest runner

Ninth batter The best bunter

Bunt

This is a tactical move used many times in baseball, when a batter, by moving one hand up the bat, pushes the ball with a dead bat. As a result the ball rolls

The batter here lays down a bunt to progress runners around the bases

slowly in the infield or down the lines, creating fielding problems for the defensive team and allowing the baserunners time to score.

Bunting is a very important part of the offensive tactics of a team. It is used both to advance a runner or runners and to make a base hit. The most common situation in which the bunt is used is when the team at bat have a man on third base in a scoring position with less then two men out. Bunting requires skill and self-confidence.

Squeeze play

Squeeze play is an offensive tactic whereby the batting team scores a run by using a particular play, e.g. a 'sacrifice bunt'. A batter makes such a sacrifice, i.e. deliberately getting himself dismissed, in order for baserunners to advance or score.

Substitution

The manager of the offensive team may change the player at bat for a substitute hitter, for example, when a hit is badly needed. The original batter is then out of the remaining part of the game. The substitute, known as a pinch hitter, is often substituted before he fields. The manager may similarly bring on a pinch runner.

A designated hitter bats in place of the pitcher in the batting order. This is allowed in some leagues only.

Hit and run

This tactic is designed to move players around the diamond when there is a runner on first base and there are less than two players out. The batter has to hit the ball and on the hit the runners all advance. The runner on first base starts towards second base to give the impression of stealing across. The fielders are drawn to second base to cover, and the batter hits the ball into the spaces that have been vacated by the fielders.

This tactic forces the batter to hit the ball and helps prevent the double-play. Its success depends upon the batter and the runners acknowledging by a signal that they are aware of the play. A missed signal is disastrous and gives the defensive side a double or even a triple-play to end the innings.

This pitcher demonstrates great style in ▶ his delivery

Glossary

During the long history of baseball, a language has emerged that explains the rules. It is a combination of terms to describe official match situations and colourful slang expressions that have now been accepted as part of the sport's terminology.

The following list includes in the main only those terms which are not mentioned elsewhere in the text. While it is not fully comprehensive, it should help the reader's understanding and enjoyment of the game.

Bleachers The cheapest seats at a baseball ground, not covered by a stand; the sun shines on them and they 'bleach'.

Bottom The second half of each inning, when the home team is at bat.

Choke A batter moving his hands down the bat handle.

Cut-off man A fielder who intercepts a thrown ball, usually from the outfield, allowing a greater chance of dismissing baserunners advancing around the diamond.

Double A fair, batted ball that allows the hitter to reach second base.

Double-header Two games played by the same teams, the second game starting immediately the first game is completed.

Fair ball A batted ball that lands in fair territory.

Foul ball A batted ball that lands in foul territory.

Foul tip A batted ball that travels straight to the catcher and is caught. Foul tips are counted as strikes.

Grand slam When a batter hits a home run with all bases occupied, and scores four runs.

Ground out A ball hit along the ground which is fielded by an infielder and is thrown to first base to make an 'out'.

Ground rules Rules appertaining to the field where the game is played, that make allowances and awards and set the number of bases. For example, a ball into a short right field could be a ground rule double.

Hop The bounce of a ball that is hit into the ground.

Hot box When the defensive team traps a baserunner between bases.

Interference This occurs in many ways, e.g. if a batter impedes the catcher from making a play; if the baserunner obstructs the defence in fielding or throwing the ball; if the umpire accidentally impedes the defence; or if a spectator touches the ball while it is in play. The umpire decides on the penalty or award to be made to the relevant team.

Line drive A ball hit fiercely by a batter that travels at high speed, without touching the ground, in a direct line to a fielder.

Live ball Any ball that is in play.

Losing pitcher The pitcher who is pitching when the offensive side scores the runs necessary to keep ahead and win.

No hitter A game in which the pitcher concedes no 'safe hits' to the offensive team batters.

Obstruction When a member of the fielding side, who does not have the ball in his possession and is not directly involved in the play, deliberately hinders any advancing baserunner.

Pick-up When a fielder cleanly collects a ball from the ground and then throws to another fielder.

All eyes are on the ball here as the batter hits a home run

Pop-fly A ball that is hit very high, but comes down in the infield and is caught.
Raincheck If a game is rained off, the spectators are issued a ticket for admission to the re-arranged game.
Relief pitcher A pitcher who substitutes for the pitcher in the starting line-up.
Retouch the bases A baserunner must return and touch the base he occupied when a hit was made if it is illegal for some reason, e.g. a foul hit.
Run-down When a baserunner is trapped between bases in a 'hot box'. The defensive side tries to touch the runner with the ball, and the runner attempts to avoid it.
Safe hit A batted ball that earns the batter a base or bases without a fielder's error.
Seventh innings stretch This occurs in American Major League games between the halves of the seventh inning, when spectators refresh themselves. It is similar to the half-time interval in soccer or rugby.
Shutout When the opposing team scores no runs.
Substitution When a player is replaced (which can happen at any time

during a game), he cannot take any further part in that game.
Tag When a fielder touches a base while holding the ball; or touches a runner with the ball or with his hands holding the ball.
Tag-out When a fielder, holding the ball in his hand or glove, touches a runner who is between bases or who is off his basc whilc thc ball is in play.
Texas leaguer A ball that drops between the infielders and outfielders.
Top The first half of each inning.
Triple A fair hit that allows the batter/runner to safely reach third base.
Wild pitch A ball delivered by the pitcher to the batter that is so wide of the strike zone, the catcher can neither stop nor block the pitched ball.

Fig. 12 An official league softball

Softball

Fundamentals of the game

The game of softball was derived from baseball; it was played indoors as early as 1887. The rules were standardised in 1933, and the game has increased in popularity ever since. Until the 1960s softball was played mainly by women, but there are now many mixed and male teams.

The governing bodies of baseball and softball work closely together, particularly in promoting the sports at international level. They have much in common: the basic concept of both is to move runners around the bases and to score runs.

There are some differences between baseball and softball. They include the dimensions of the playing area and the size of the bat and ball. The toss of a coin determines which softball team bats first, and a game consists of seven innings rather than nine. The softball pitcher throws underarm, which means that hits are more frequent than in baseball and there is even greater excitement on the bases.

There are two forms of softball: fast pitch and slow pitch. The fast pitch game has been adopted in Europe.

The playing area

The softball diamond is smaller than the baseball one, and there are different diamonds for male and female players. For fast pitch softball, the measurement between bases is 60 ft (18.3 m), and the pitching distance is 46 ft (14 m) for men and 40 ft (12.2 m) for women. For slow pitch softball, the measurement between bases is 65 ft (19.8 m) for men and 60 ft (18.3 m) for women; the pitching distance is 46 ft (14 m) for both sexes.

Other measurements that differ from baseball include the batting box, which is 3 ft (0.9 m) by 7 ft (2.1 m), the pitcher's circle (radius of 8 ft (2.4 m)), and the catcher's area (8 ft by 10 ft or 2.4 m by 3 m).

Equipment

The ball

The ball is larger and heavier than the baseball; it has a circumference of $11\frac{7}{8}$ to $12\frac{1}{8}$ in (29.9 to 31 cm) and a weight of $6\frac{1}{4}$ to 7 oz (177 to 198 g). It is manufactured in the same way as a baseball, and is certainly not soft.

The bat

The softball bat is shorter than the baseball one; it is no longer than 34 in (86.4 cm), has a maximum weight of 38 oz (1.1 kg) and a maximum diameter of $2\frac{1}{4}$ in (5.7 cm) at its thickest part. Any safety grip on the bat must not extend further than 15 in (38.1 cm) down the handle.

Protective equipment

All equipment is the same as in baseball, except that the gloves of the fielding side are larger to allow for the larger ball.

Fig. 13 An aluminium softball bat

Different versions of softball

Fast pitch softball

Of the two varieties of softball, fast pitch is the one which is more like baseball; the fielding positions are exactly the same.

The main difference between fast pitch softball and baseball lies in the pitching technique. The pitcher stands with both feet in contact with the pitching plate, and with one shoulder pointing to first base and the other to third base.

Before delivering the ball, the pitcher holds it with both hands in front of his body for not less than one second and no more than ten seconds. The ball must remain in view of the batter once one hand has been removed from it.

The pitcher uses a 'windmill pitch' to deliver the ball (underhand); one revolution is allowed, and is followed by a whip action with the wrist when the ball is released.

The pitcher is allowed to take one step forwards towards the batter when delivering the ball. It is released below the hip, and the wrist should be no further from the body than the elbow.

The strike-zone in fast pitch softball is the same as in baseball.

Slow pitch softball

The basic concept of the slow pitch game is the same as in fast pitch softball and baseball. The main differences are as follows.

1. Each team has ten players; the extra player fields in the infield and is known as a short-fielder.
2. Stealing from one base to another is not allowed. A runner cannot leave his base until the ball passes over home plate.
3. The pitcher delivers the ball in an underhand arc; the ball must be no higher than 6–12 ft (1.83–3.66 m) from the ground at the top of the arc. The ball must be thrown at a moderate speed; a pitcher who throws it very fast risks dismissal from the match.
4. The strike-zone is more generous than in fast pitch softball and baseball; it stretches from the top of the knee to the higher shoulder.

Tee-ball

Tee-ball is a game that can be used as a basic introduction to the sports of baseball and softball. It is aimed at schoolchildren, but can be enjoyed by people of all ages.

Fundamentals of the game

The number of players in a team is flexible, but nine in each side is recommended.

The ball is placed on a tee, which stands at about chest height. Each player on the batting side comes up to the tee in rotation for a turn at bat. The batter tries to hit the ball off the tee into fair territory and reach the bases before the ball is thrown to a baseman. The following batters do the same, thus moving runners around the bases to cross the home plate and score a run.

The object of the fielding side, as in baseball and softball, is to gain three outs; dismissals are gained in the same way as in the other two sports.

When the last batter comes to the tee, all baserunners must run; the inning is closed after this, irrespective of how many outs the fielding side has gained. It is then the turn of the fielding side to bat; when each side has batted, one inning is concluded.

The game continues either until the end of a fixed time limit or until a predetermined number of innings have been completed.

The playing area

Tee-ball can be played indoors or outdoors. The playing area can be tailored to the space available, but the International Baseball Association suggests the following dimensions, linked to specific age groups.

Age 8–10 Distance between bases: 60 ft (18.3 m)
Distance home (tee) to pitcher: 46 ft (14 m)

Age 6–8 Distance between bases: 45 ft (13.7 m)
Distance home (tee) to pitcher: 35 ft (10.6 m)

Fig. 14 The tee-ball stand

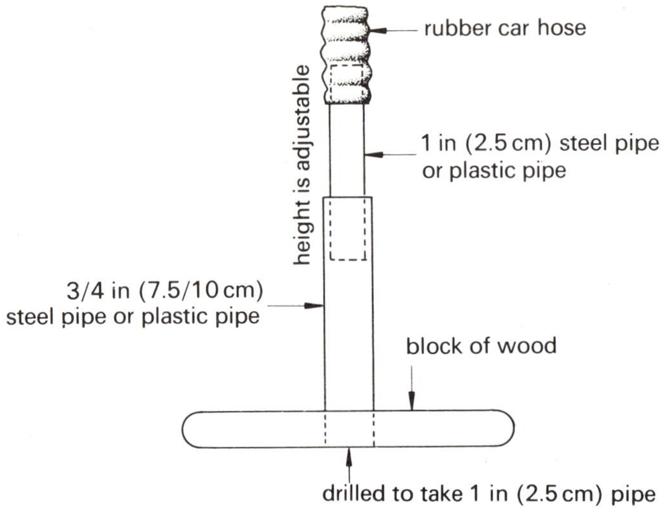

Equipment

The equipment required is inexpensive, and can be home-made.

The tee-ball stand

There are several types of stand, all of which may be easily made or purchased.

Clothing

Players should wear comfortable clothing, bearing in mind whether they are playing indoors or outdoors. A T-shirt and track suit bottoms or jeans are ideal while training shoes make excellent footwear. A baseball cap, while not essential, is part of the game of baseball and adds to the fun.

The ball

The type of ball used depends on whether or not the fielders have gloves. If gloves are not available, a tennis ball or, for greater safety, a punctured tennis ball may be used so as not to injure the fielders. If gloves are available then specially manufactured balls may be used.

Playing positions

The pitcher (1)

In tee-ball the pitcher acts only as a fielder.

The catcher (2)

The catcher is the fielder who looks after the home plate.

First baseman (3)

This fielder is responsible for looking after first base and the right-hand side of the infield.

Second baseman (4)

The same as for the first baseman, only at second base.

Shortstop (6)

This player has the same responsibilities as the second baseman.

Third baseman (5)

The third baseman looks after third base and the left-hand side of the infield.

Right field, centre field and left field (7, 8 and 9)

These three fielders man the outfield.

The batting side

These players sit away from the field in batting order until their turn at bat comes around. The batter then stands either to the left or to the right of the tee, depending on whether he is left or right-handed.

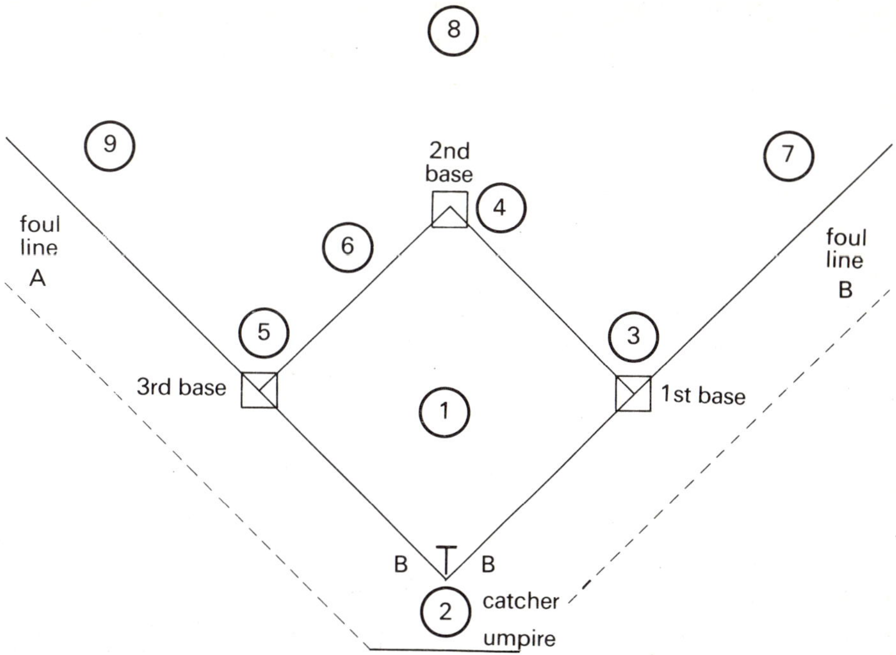

Fig. 15 Playing positions for tee-ball

Index

The Dodgers' stadium in Los Angeles ▶